Smelling Things

By Allan Fowler

Images supplied by VALAN Photos

Consultants:

Robert L. Hillerich, Ph.D., Bowling Green
State University, Bowling Green, Ohio

Mary Nalbandian, Director of Science,
Chicago Public Schools, Chicago, Illinois

Fay Robinson, Child Development Specialist

CHILDRENS PRESS®

CHICAGO

Series Cover and interior design by Sara Shelton

Library of Congress Cataloging-in-Publication Data

Fowler, Allan.
    Smelling things / by Allan Fowler.
       p.   cm.—(Rookie read-about science)
    Summary: A simple introduction to the sense of smell.
    ISBN 0-516-04912-7
    1. Smell—Juvenile literature. [1. Smell. 2. Senses and
sensation.] I. Title. II. Series.
QP458.F68 1991   90-22123
                                            CIP
                                            AC

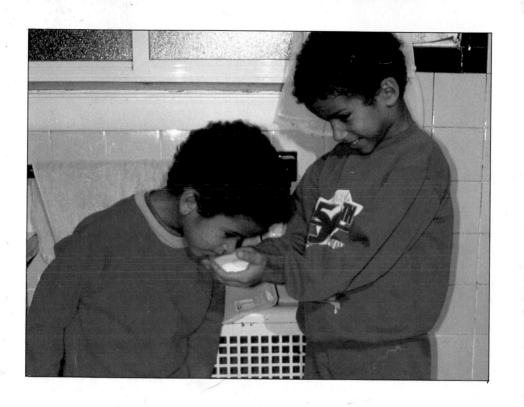

Let's say your eyes are
closed and a friend holds
a bar of soap close to
your nose.

Or someone holds a handful of newly cut grass.

Could you tell which is
which?

Sure you could.

How do you know?
Your nose tells you.

Try it.

You are using your sense of smell.

You have five senses.
The others are seeing,

hearing,

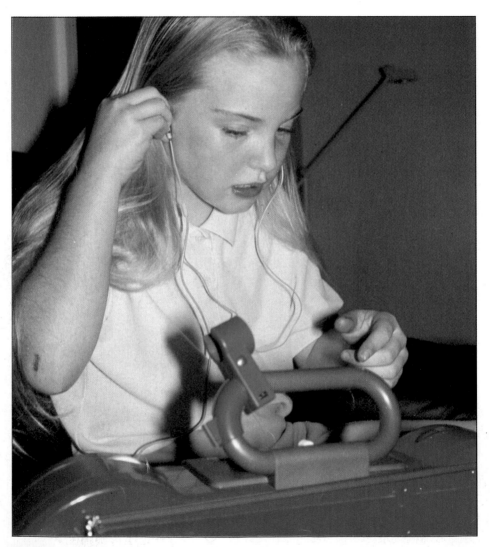

feeling,

and tasting.

Smell and taste often go together.

The chicken smells good while it's roasting. So you know it will taste good too.

13

Did you ever walk past a bakery and smell something so good that you just had to go inside?

You were smelling the delicious aromas of bread and pastries fresh from the oven.

15

A bouquet of flowers can smell as fresh as it looks.

Sometimes you can tell where you are by what your nose tells you.

There's a fresh, clean
smell in a forest of pine
trees.

And a salty smell near the ocean.

Sniff the fresh air after a rainshower.

How do you like the smell of blue cheese?

How do you like the
smell of popcorn?

A dog has a very keen sense of smell. It can tell its owner's smell apart from anyone else's.

A dog's sense of smell can
even help find people
who get lost.

Your sense of smell can help you keep out of trouble.

It warns you if there's a
skunk around, or if
something's burning.

Even if you don't see what's out there, your nose knows!

Words You Know

sense of smell

aroma

bakery

blue cheese

bouquet of
flowers

forest

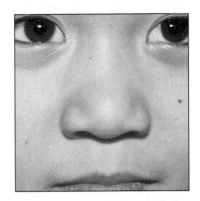

nose

ocean

skunk

Index

About the Author

Allan Fowler is a free-lance writer with a background in advertising. Born in New York, he lives in Chicago now and enjoys traveling.

Photo Credits

Valan—© Murray O'Neill, Cover; © V. Wilkinson, 3, 4, 8, 13, 22, 23, 30 (bottom left), 31 (top right); © Kennon Cooke, 7, 15, 16, 30 (top left, top right, bottom right); © Wouterloot-Gregoire, 9; © V. Whelan, 10; © Val & Alan Wilkinson, 19, 31 (top left); © Pierre Kohler, 20, 31 (bottom left); © Dr. A. Farquhar, 21; © J.A. Wilkinson, 25; © Herman H. Giethoorn, 26; © Wayne Lankinen, 28, 31 (bottom right)

COVER: Striped skunk